MICHELANGELO

First published in North America in 2006 by the
National Geographic Society
1145 17th Street N.W.
Washington, D.C. 20036-4688

Copyright © 2006 Marshall Editions
A Marshall Edition
Conceived, edited, and designed by Marshall Editions
The Old Brewery, 6 Blundell Street, London N7 9BH, U.K.
www.quarto.com

Trade ISBN: 0-7922-5533-X
Library ISBN: 0-7922-5534-8
Library of Congress Cataloging-in-Publication Data available on request.

Originated in Hong Kong by Modern Age
Printed and bound in China by Midas Printing Limited

Publisher: Richard Green
Commissioning editor: Claudia Martin
Art direction: Ivo Marloh
Picture manager: Veneta Bullen
Production: Anna Pauletti

Consultant: Dr. Gabriele Neher
Design and editorial: Tall Tree Ltd.
Picture research: Caroline Wood

For the National Geographic Society:
Art director: Bea Jackson
Project editor: Virginia Ann Koeth

One of the world's largest nonprofit scientific and educational organizations, the National Geographic Society
was founded in 1888 "for the increase and diffusion of geographic knowledge." Fulfilling this mission, the Society
educates and inspires millions every day through its magazines, books, television programs, videos, maps and atlases,
research grants, the National Geographic Bee, teacher workshops, and innovative classroom materials. The Society
is supported through membership dues, charitable gifts, and income from the sale of its educational products.
This support is vital to National Geographic's mission to increase global understanding and promote conservation
of our planet through exploration, research, and education.

For more information, please call 1-800-NGS LINE (647-5463) or write to the following address:

NATIONAL GEOGRAPHIC SOCIETY
1145 17th Street N.W.
Washington, D.C. 20036-4688 U.S.A.

Visit the Society's Web site at www.nationalgeographic.com.

Previous page: Michelangelo's statue of Moses forms part of the tomb of Pope Julius II in Rome.
Opposite: At the center of the ceiling of the Sistine Chapel in Rome, Michelangelo painted the
figure of God. Surrounded by angels, He is at the moment of bringing Adam to life.

MICHELANGELO

THE YOUNG ARTIST WHO
DREAMED OF PERFECTION

PHILIP WILKINSON

NATIONAL GEOGRAPHIC

WASHINGTON, D.C.

CONTENTS

TOWN BOY, COUNTRY BOY

1

THE YOUNG SCULPTOR

2

ARTIST TO THE POPE

3

THE LATER YEARS

4

TOWN BOY, COUNTRY BOY

1

The Magistrate's Son

In the early hours of March 6, 1475, in the small town of Caprese near Florence in Italy, a baby boy was born. His parents, Francesca and Lodovico di Lionardi Buonarroti Simoni, who normally shortened their family name to Buonarroti, called their son Michelangelo. The boy was to become one of the most famous names in the history of art.

Michelangelo's father was from a well-to-do family that had lost most of its money. The family had been wool merchants and bankers in Florence, but by the time Michelangelo's grandfather was head of the business, it was losing money and eventually collapsed. Lodovico ran a farm outside Florence and had a house in the city, but very little else. When the Buonarroti's first child, Leonardo, was born in 1473, Lodovico had to get a job.

So in 1474, he took the post of *podestà* (magistrate) in the towns of Chiusi and Caprese. The podestà was an important person in the town where he served. Lodovico and his family moved to a large stone house in the middle of Caprese. Here Michelangelo was born.

Previous page: This delicate chalk drawing of a young boy was done by Michelangelo in the 1530s.

Left: The Buonarroti home in Caprese was a typical Italian country house. The living rooms were on the upper floor, reached by an outside staircase.

1472
Lodovico di Lionardi Buonarroti Simoni, a 28-year-old man of noble family from Florence, marries Francesca di Neri.

1474
Lodovico is appointed podestà for the Italian towns of Chiusi and Caprese.

In the 15th century, upper-class women were not expected to look after their children themselves. They had servants to do most of the work, and small children often lived with a woman called a wet nurse, someone who had recently borne children herself and could breast-feed a baby. Michelangelo was sent to live with a wet nurse who also lived in Caprese. She was married to a stonecutter, and when Michelangelo later became a sculptor, he said that he had drunk marble dust with his nurse's milk.

Above: The countryside around Florence was dotted with small walled towns surrounded by fields where olives and corn grew.

As a boy, Michelangelo might have played soccer using a stuffed pig's bladder, or ball games like bowling with the local children. At home, he would have amused himself with simple toys like spinning tops. There would have been plenty for an observant child like Michelangelo to look at in the stone-cutter's workshop. Perhaps the stone-cutter made toy soldiers for him from offcuts of marble. The magistrate's son seemed destined to spend a quiet life in a small country town.

The podestà's role

The podestà was both mayor and judge. The towns around Florence usually chose an outsider to be a podestà. People thought that a local man might favor his friends when making judgments in court.

March 6, 1475

Michelangelo di Lodovico di Lionardi Buonarroti Simoni is born at Caprese.

1475

Michelangelo is taken to a wet nurse. He probably stays with his nurse for about three years.

A Boy in Florence

After a few years with his nurse, Michelangelo returned to his family. By 1481, he had three younger brothers, Buonarroto, Giovansimone, and Gismondo. Lodovico's term as podestà had come to an end and he resumed his career as a merchant. The family was back in their house in Florence's Santa Croce district. In 1481, Michelangelo's mother died. For a seven-year-old, this must have been a devastating blow.

Above: In the church of Santa Croce, Michelangelo could see this crucifix made by Donatello, the greatest Italian sculptor of the 15th century.

Florence was one of the richest of the Italian cities, making its money mainly from banking and the cloth trade. Like the other Italian cities, it was a small independent state, officially governed by the *Signoria*, a group of its most prominent citizens. In practice, the Signoria was dominated by the most powerful family, the Medici. Santa Croce, named after the church at its center, was a bustling neighborhood in the middle of Florence's wool-trading district. All sorts of people gathered there—merchants and money-changers discussing business, craftworkers hurrying to their looms, and beggars on street corners.

1477 and 1479
Michelangelo's brothers Buonarroto and Giovansimone are born.

1481
Michelangelo's mother, Francesca, dies soon after the birth of his fourth brother, Gismondo.

Calcio in the piazza

An early Italian ball game, calcio was a struggle between two teams to get hold of a ball. The game was originally played with a cannon ball and the danger as the heavy ball flew around was part of the excitement. There were few rules and the game was full of violent scuffles.

Sometimes, the square in front of the church was cleared for entertainment and games. Occasionally there was a tournament, when knights fought on horseback with lances or on foot with swords. On other occasions there were ball games, such as the rough game called *calcio*.

Every Sunday, Michelangelo's family went to Mass at the church of Santa Croce, which was full of some of the best works of art of the period. These included a crucifix carved by the famous sculptor Donatello and wall paintings by Giotto, one of the greatest artists of all time. Michelangelo must have marveled at these works and at the rich citizens who had employed the artists who made them. These works of art helped the priests teach ordinary people, who could not read or write, about the Christian faith.

At home, things began to look up. In 1485, Lodovico remarried. His new wife, Lucrezia, came from a rich family and brought with her 600 florins, an enormous sum of money, as a dowry. As the son of wealthy parents, Michelangelo seemed likely to have a good career.

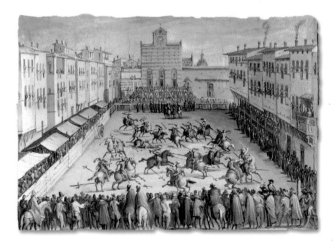

Right: This painting by Vasari shows a tournament at Santa Croce.

August 29, 1484

Innocent VIII is elected pope. Lorenzo de' Medici sends his son Piero to offer his congratulations.

1485

Lodovico remarries. His new wife, Lucrezia degli Ubaldini da Gagliano, brings a large dowry to the marriage.

The Renaissance in Italy

In the 14th and 15th centuries, a new artistic movement saw artists starting to look more closely at the classical cultures of ancient Greece and Rome. This movement became known as the Renaissance, from a French word meaning "rebirth." Inspired by the realism and beauty of ancient sculpture and architecture, artists began to change the way they worked. Before the Renaissance, there was not much sense of depth, or perspective, in paintings—figures and scenery looked flat. Medieval pictures also lacked scale—the most important figures were shown largest, in spite of how big they were in reality. By developing a sense of scale and using techniques like shading and perspective, Renaissance artists made their works look realistic.

Milan • Verona Venice

Mantua • Padua

Parma • Ferrara

Genoa • Bologna

Carrara •

Lucca • Rimini

Pisa • Florence

Chiusi

Caprese • Urbino

Siena

Assisi

Adriatic Sea

Rome

N
W · E
S

Left: The cathedrals of the Middle Ages had towers, but in the Renaissance, architects began to build domes as the Romans had done. The cathedral in Florence was started in 1296, but for more than a century no one could figure out how to build a dome big enough to cover its central space. The man who succeeded was the architect Filippo Brunelleschi. His dome was called one of the wonders of the world when it was finished in 1436.

Above: The Florentine artist Sandro Botticelli painted "Primavera" (Spring) in the 1470s, around the time when Michelangelo was born. Botticelli's style is much more naturalistic than earlier works of art, with realistic faces, flowing fabric, and a sense that the figures are three-dimensional.

LEONARDO

The only figure of the Renaissance who rivaled Michelangelo in the scope of his genius was Leonardo da Vinci (1452–1519). A master of painting and drawing, Leonardo did not share Michelangelo's genius for sculpture or poetry.

However, Leonardo was a remarkable inventor, and his notebooks are full of drawings of extraordinary machines. These sketches included flying machines, cannon, and this catapult, based on the design of a crossbow.

Grammar School

Above: Students in the 15th century sit at their desks reading. Scholars studied the Latin authors of the Roman period and translated their works.

In the 15th century, most children did not go to school. Girls helped their mothers at home, while boys worked alongside their fathers. Things were different in a merchant's family—education was important for business. So when Michelangelo was nine, his father sent him to school.

Michelangelo went to a grammar school run by a teacher named Francesco da Urbino. The aim of his education was to learn Latin, which was the language of business and government. So most of Michelangelo's time at school was spent reading and translating the works of ancient Rome. Michelangelo also learned to write in Latin and may have learned how to write Latin poetry. Since most artists never went to school to learn Latin, Michelangelo's education gave him an advantage later in his life. He was intelligent and had beautiful handwriting. He admired the writings of the authors he had to translate, especially the poets. He would love poetry for the rest of his life. However, according to his pupil and biographer Ascanio Condivi, who wrote about him 70 years later, Michelangelo was bored with his studies. He really wanted to draw instead.

1485
Under Lorenzo de' Medici, the influence of Florence continues to rise, as the city becomes the most powerful in Italy.

1485
Michelangelo learns Latin at the grammar school in Florence run by teacher Francesco da Urbino.

> *"Whenever he was able to steal some time, he could not resist running off to draw in one place or another, and seeking out the company of painters."*
>
> Ascanio Condivi, *Life of Michelangelo Buonarroti*, 1553

When Michelangelo told his father about his interest in art, Lodovico was not impressed. In 15th-century Italy, artists were seen as the servants of noblemen. They were not very well paid and were usually expected to mix with the other servants. Also, artists were not expected to have ideas of their own. Instead, the patron (employer) would ask for a picture or carving of a subject, and it would be the artist's job to produce the work of art. Lodovico wanted a better life for his son, and he forced Michelangelo to continue with his schooling.

One person who understood Michelangelo's love of drawing was an older boy named Francesco Granacci whom Michelangelo spent time with. Granacci was an apprentice to the famous artist Domenico Ghirlandaio. He showed Michelangelo the work of other artists and took the boy to Ghirlandaio's workshop. Michelangelo was convinced that he wanted to be an artist too.

Learning Latin

Today, it is unusual to be bilingual (able to speak two languages well), but in the Renaissance, educated people were expected to be able to speak, read, and write Latin as well as their own local tongue. Latin allowed traders, diplomats, and churchmen to speak to people from any European country and to write documents that all educated people could understand.

1486

Michelangelo becomes friendly with Francesco Granacci, who is five years older and an apprentice painter.

1486–90

The painters of Ghirlandaio's workshop are busy with wall paintings for the church of Santa Maria Novella.

The Workshop

Michelangelo kept begging his father to let him become an artist. Even as a boy, he knew what he wanted to do and had a strong will to achieve his goal. Granacci, meanwhile, showed his master some of the boy's drawings, and Ghirlandaio was impressed. In the end, Lodovico gave in. In 1488, at the age of 12, Michelangelo became an apprentice to Ghirlandaio.

The workshop was the most successful in Florence. Domenico Ghirlandaio and his brothers, Davide and Benedetto, had produced paintings for the pope in Rome and now had lots of work decorating churches in Florence. Their biggest project was a series of murals for the church of Santa Maria Novella. They had a number of apprentices, between 8 and 15 years old, living with them and helping them on murals and panel paintings. At 12, Michelangelo was quite old to start as an apprentice. As was usual, Lodovico paid Ghirlandaio for living expenses and training.

Right: When Domenico Ghirlandaio painted the altarpiece in the church of Santa Trinità in Florence, he included this self-portrait among the figures.

1487
Michelangelo begins to go to the workshop of the Florentine painter Domenico Ghirlandaio.

1488
Lodovico signs a formal agreement that his son will serve a three-year apprenticeship with Ghirlandaio.

Left: This is one of Ghirlandaio's wall-paintings in the church of Santa Maria Novella in Florence. In a large, complex painting like this, Ghirlandaio would have painted the figures, but areas such as the buildings, trees, and sky would have been done by the apprentices.

The Ghirlandaio brothers showed the apprentices how to prepare a wooden panel for painting and how to plaster a wall ready for the painting of a fresco. They were shown how to make paints. They also learned the art of making working drawings, called cartoons, on which finished paintings would be based.

Frescoes

Michelangelo's paintings in the Sistine Chapel are frescoes. This term comes from an Italian word meaning "fresh," and it refers to the fact that the paint is applied when the top layer of plaster is still damp. When the artist puts on the paint, which is mixed with water, the pigment combines with the plaster, making a very long-lasting image.

Michelangelo was fascinated by the appearance of everything around him. When doing a drawing of some monsters, he copied the scales of fish in the local market. His work was so good that Ghirlandaio began to grow jealous of his pupil's talent. Michelangelo was also getting restless. He started to become interested in sculpture, but there was no way he could learn how to carve in a painter's workshop.

1488
Working with Ghirlandaio, Michelangelo meets many of the rich Florentines who will later become his patrons.

1488
Michelangelo produces a number of drawings by copying the work of older Italian artists such as Masaccio.

THE YOUNG
SCULPTOR

2

In the Sculpture Garden

Above: Even when he was studying sculpture, Michelangelo continued to copy the works of great painters. He made this drawing of part of a fresco by the great painter Giotto in his local church of Santa Croce in Florence.

Previous page: Giuliano Bugiardini's portrait shows Michelangelo as a young man wearing a fashionable turban on his head.

Some of the most important people in Florence visited Ghirlandaio's workshop—some visitors were members of the household of Lorenzo de' Medici, the most powerful man in the city. Before long, Michelangelo met a number of these people, and one of them, an old sculptor named Bertoldo di Giovanni, was soon to change the young artist's life.

As a young man, Bertoldo had been a pupil of the great sculptor Donatello. Now he was employed by Lorenzo de' Medici to make statues and medals and to look after Lorenzo's art collection. Many of Lorenzo's statues were displayed in a garden where artists went to draw and carve. Student sculptors often went there, and Bertoldo advised them about their work. Bertoldo encouraged the young Michelangelo to join them in the garden.

1489
Michelangelo is befriended by the elderly sculptor Bertoldo di Giovanni.

1489
Michelangelo begins to go to the sculpture garden owned by Lorenzo de' Medici.

Copying the ancients

In Michelangelo's time, people thought that the best sculptors were the ancient Greeks and Romans because they were so good at showing the human figure. The Medici garden contained some of the finest of these ancient sculptures, and many artists came to copy them.

Before long, Michelangelo left Ghirlandaio's workshop for good. He started making sculptures by modeling in clay.

The garden was not far from the Medici palace, and artists came there in the hope that their talent would be spotted by Lorenzo. He soon noticed Michelangelo's ability, even though he was only 15. This made other sculptors in the garden jealous.

One of these, Pietro Torrigiano, often picked quarrels with Michelangelo. The two fought, and Michelangelo's nose was broken. Pietro said that Michelangelo would have his "signature" on him for the rest of his life.

Michelangelo soon got over the pain, however. Around this time he begged a spare piece of marble—which was very expensive—from another sculptor and created his first carving: the head of a faun, a mischievous figure from ancient Roman myths. Lorenzo was impressed by this carving.

Right: One of the sculptures that inspired Michelangelo was Bertoldo's relief of a battle displayed in the Medici palace. Bertoldo probably made the relief in or around the year of Michelangelo's birth.

1490
Michelangelo quarrels with Pietro Torrigiano, who breaks the young artist's nose.

1490
Michelangelo begs a spare piece of marble and carves his first sculpture, a head of a faun, which is now lost.

The Medici

In the 13th century, a family called the Medici made a great deal of money through trade and banking in Florence. Their money allowed them to take positions of power in the city. By the time Michelangelo was born, they had reached the height of their power under Lorenzo de' Medici (1449–92). He was known as "Lorenzo the Magnificent" because of his wealth and love of luxury. However, Medici power was always under threat. During the 16th century, a series of conflicts known as the Italian Wars saw the Italian cities threatened by outside forces who wanted their wealth. On several occasions, the Medici and their supporters had to run from the city in fear for their lives.

Above: This coin shows Cosimo de' Medici (1389–1464), the first of the Medici to rule Florence, which he did for 30 years.

Below: Renaissance artists often included portraits of their patrons in their work. In Sandro Botticelli's "Adoration of the Magi," the three kings (center, kneeling) who bring gifts to Jesus are members of the Medici family: Cosimo, Lorenzo, and Giuliano.

SEAT OF POWER

The Palazzo della Signoria was the town hall of Florence. In the 15th century, it was the headquarters of the city's rulers and where the Medici dispensed justice to their people. Many of the rooms were magnificently decorated by the best artists. Although plans for frescoes by Leonardo and Michelangelo came to nothing, decorations like the paintings in the Hall of Lorenzo (shown here), by Vasari, still survive.

Right: Lorenzo's son Piero (1473–1503) took over the government after his father in 1492. He was forced out of the city by angry Florentines when he negotiated with attacking French forces.

Professional Sculptor

By the time he was 15, the young sculptor had been given his own room in the Medici palace. Lorenzo was impressed with his ability and paid him an allowance. Everyone could see that Michelangelo had been singled out as someone with special abilities.

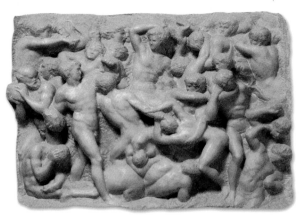

Above: In 1491–92 Michelangelo carved this action-packed battle between centaurs and people.

Above: Michelangelo's "Madonna of the Steps" is carved with very little depth. He used a style called *rilievo schiacciato* (squashed relief).

Things were now more peaceful in the sculpture garden. Pietro Torrigiano, guilty about the way he had attacked Michelangelo, fled to Rome. So Michelangelo settled down to perfect his art. He still did lots of drawings and worked hard at his carvings in marble. One of his early subjects was the idea of one of Michelangelo's colleagues in the Medici household. Agnolo Poliziano was the tutor of Lorenzo's children. He suggested that Michelangelo carve a scene from mythology: the battle of the centaurs. Centaurs were monsters with the heads and arms of men and the bodies of horses. It was a scene with lots of fighting that gave Michelangelo a chance to show action.

1490
Michelangelo becomes a member of the household of Lorenzo de' Medici.

1490
Lorenzo refurbishes the Medici library, giving his family access to the best of Renaissance learning and literature.

Very different was a small work called the "Madonna of the Steps." It shows the Virgin Mary nursing the infant Jesus. Like the "Battle of the Centaurs," it was a relief panel. Reliefs are carved from flat surfaces of stone, so that the figures are not totally three-dimensional. Although Michelangelo never finished the figures in the background, the sculpture shows that he could already carve with amazing realism and gentleness.

Dressing up

In 15th-century Italy, rich men like Lorenzo treated their artists as servants and made them wear servants' clothes. When Michelangelo went to live in Lorenzo's palace, he was given a cloak of rich purple cloth—a sign that the young sculptor was special.

Things could not have been better for Michelangelo. He had a cultured employer who valued his talent. Florence was an exciting city in which to live and work. But not everyone was so happy with how things were. In 1491, a fierce friar named Girolamo Savonarola became prior of the monastery of San Marco in Florence. He preached against the Medici and their vast wealth, predicting that they would soon fall from power. People began to worry.

Left: Michelangelo's first carving, the head of a faun, has been lost, but it is shown in this 17th-century painting, in which Lorenzo de' Medici (center) and a group of artists admire the carving. The young Michelangelo is shown on the far right, listening to his employer's opinion of his work.

1491
Michelangelo carves the "Madonna of the Steps."

1491–92
Michelangelo carves the "Battle of the Centaurs," showing a fight between the ancient Greeks and mythical beasts.

The Death of Lorenzo

By 1492, Michelangelo was a successful young sculptor. He was just 17 years old and had a powerful patron. That April, however, Lorenzo died. Piero, his son, took over, but he cared little for sculpture. Meanwhile, Savonarola was still preaching doom for Florence. The pope died that same year, throwing Rome into confusion, too.

The young sculptor was saddened at Lorenzo's death. He had lost a friend as well as an employer. For days he did not feel like working, but eventually he bought a block of marble and began to carve a statue of the mythological hero Hercules. Piero gave Michelangelo no work until the winter. When the snow was thick on the ground, Piero decided he would like a snowman and ordered Michelangelo to make one. It was the artist's strangest commission.

Around this time, the prior of Santo Spirito asked Michelangelo to make a crucifix for the church. Pleased with the end result, the prior gave Michelangelo the use of a room in which the artist could work.

Right: Venice in the late 15th century was a busy city. Among the many artists working there was Gentile Bellini, who painted this view of the city.

April 8, 1492	July 11, 1492
Lorenzo dies, leaving Michelangelo without a patron.	Alexander VI, a member of the powerful Borgia family, is elected pope.

Here he could dissect (cut up) corpses to study anatomy. Michelangelo was determined that if he was going to make sculptures of the human body he should know exactly how it was put together. He was one of the first people to dissect and study the human body in this way.

In 1494, Florence faced another problem—an army led by King Charles VIII of France was at the walls threatening to overrun the city. Many people, including Michelangelo, fled Florence. He traveled to Bologna in northern Italy, and then on to Venice. At the time, Venice was an important trading city, and Michelangelo hoped to find work. However, no work could be found, so he went back to Bologna.

Here Michelangelo met an important citizen and politician named Gian Francesco Aldovrandi. He showed Michelangelo the unfinished shrine of San Domenico in the church of the same name. He asked the artist if he would carve the missing figures—two saints and an angel. At last, Michelangelo was busy again. Back in Florence, the Medici had fled, leaving the prior Savonarola free to take power.

Above: Savonarola became very influential with his sermons criticizing the Medici. For a while, after the Medici were driven from power, he became ruler of Florence.

Lives of luxury

The Medici were so rich they could live as luxuriously as kings and queens in other European countries. They had houses throughout northern Italy, and they employed the greatest artists of the time to decorate them. However, they were also guilty of corruption. They used state money to prop up their businesses and to keep up their rich lifestyle.

September 21, 1492
Savonarola preaches a sermon predicting doom for the city of Florence.

October 1494
With Florence under threat from French troops, Michelangelo leaves the city for Bologna and Venice.

Working in Rome

While Michelangelo worked in Bologna, Florence was in trouble. During 1495, Savonarola became the most powerful man in the city. As a strict churchman, he disapproved of books that contained new ideas and of paintings that showed the naked human body. The prospects for an artist did not look good, but Michelangelo desperately wanted to return to Florence to see his family.

When he arrived home, Michelangelo made contact with some members of the Medici family who were living under a different name to avoid persecution. He was given some work, and one of his contacts, Lorenzo di Pierfrancesco de' Medici, helped him sell one of his statues. It was a figure of the ancient Roman god of love, Cupid. Lorenzo thought it would sell well in Rome if Michelangelo treated it to look like an ancient statue. Michelangelo smeared it with dirt to make it look as if it had been buried. He then took it to Rome, the headquarters of the church. The statue, now a forged antique, impressed everyone who saw it.

Right: By Michelangelo's time, Rome was already a large city on the banks of the River Tiber. The Castel Sant' Angelo (center, with a flag on its roof), the stronghold of the popes, overlooked the city.

April 1495
Venice, Milan, Rome, and the Holy Roman Empire (Germany and Spain) form a league against the French.

June 25, 1496
Michelangelo arrives in Rome and starts working for Cardinal Riario.

The statue was bought by one of the most senior churchmen, Cardinal Raffaelle Riario.

After meeting the cardinal, Michelangelo was introduced to some very powerful people, such as the Borgia family, which included a number of senior churchmen as well as the pope. Cardinal Riario, who by now knew that Michelangelo himself had carved "Cupid," asked him to make another sculpture for his collection. Michelangelo replied that, although it might not be as good as the pieces the cardinal already possessed, he would try. Soon he was creating a statue of Bacchus, the Greek god of wine and celebrations— his first masterpiece. Everyone, except the cardinal, was impressed with the statue. He thought the god looked too drunk and did not want to pay for the statue.

Just when Michelangelo was struggling to get payment for his work, he received bad news—his father was also short of money. Michelangelo desperately needed a new patron to support himself and his family.

Above: The people of Michelangelo's time liked his "Bacchus" because it was just like an ancient statue of the god.

> *"Then the cardinal asked if I had it in me to undertake some beautiful work myself. I replied that I might not make such splendid works as he possessed, but we would see what I could do."*
>
> **Michelangelo, in a letter to Lorenzo di Pierfrancesco de' Medici, July 2, 1496, before starting work on "Bacchus"**

July 1496
Michelangelo begins to carve the statue of Bacchus, which has been called his first masterpiece.

November 1497
Michelangelo makes a trip to Carrara to search for a suitable block of marble for his new sculpture, the "Pietà."

Fame at Last

By the age of 21, Michelangelo was a superb sculptor, but he had plenty of problems. He had made little money from his "Cupid" and "Bacchus" statues; he did not have a patron; and his family was asking him for money. He badly needed to produce a large sculpture that would make him famous.

In August 1497, Michelangelo's brother Buonarroto came to Rome to tell Michelangelo that their father was in trouble. A tradesman was about to have Lodovico arrested for money he owed. Michelangelo had just bought a large, expensive block of marble. A job for Piero de' Medici had fallen through as well, so the sculptor had no money. He promised his father that he would borrow some, so that the debt could be paid.

Below: Sculptors prized marble from Carrara for its pale color and good quality. There are still marble quarries in the area.

Marble

Michelangelo's favorite material was marble, because he could polish it to a beautiful, smooth surface. Michelangelo often went to the marble quarries at Carrara in the Apennine Mountains, sometimes spending months choosing the right stone.

1497–1500

Michelangelo is hard at work on his "Pietà" sculpture.

1498

Savonarola is executed in Florence, and local nobleman Piero Soderini is made *gonfalonier* (ruler) of the city.

In November things took a turn for the better. A French ambassador, Cardinal Jean Bilhères de Lagraulas, commissioned a new work from Michelangelo. It was to be a statue of the Virgin Mary cradling the dead Jesus, a subject known as the pietà.

Michelangelo took two years to complete the "Pietà," but it was worth it. The statue was displayed at the Vatican in Rome and everyone was impressed with its beauty and realism. One day, Michelangelo was present when some people from Lombardy, a region in northern Italy, were

Above: People admired the beauty of Mary in the "Pietà" and were astonished by the realism of the flesh and fabric shown in the statue.

admiring the work. One of them asked who the artist was. "Our Gobbo, from Milan," answered another. Michelangelo kept quiet, but came back and carved his name on Mary's sash. It was the only sculpture he ever signed.

The "Pietà" made Michelangelo's name. Everyone who saw it admired it, and the most powerful men in Europe wanted Michelangelo to work for them. It seemed that he would never be short of money again.

1500

This year is celebrated as a "Holy Year" in Rome. Many pilgrims come to the Vatican to see the "Pietà."

December 1500

Lodovico once more urges his son to come home to Florence.

ARTIST TO THE POPE

3

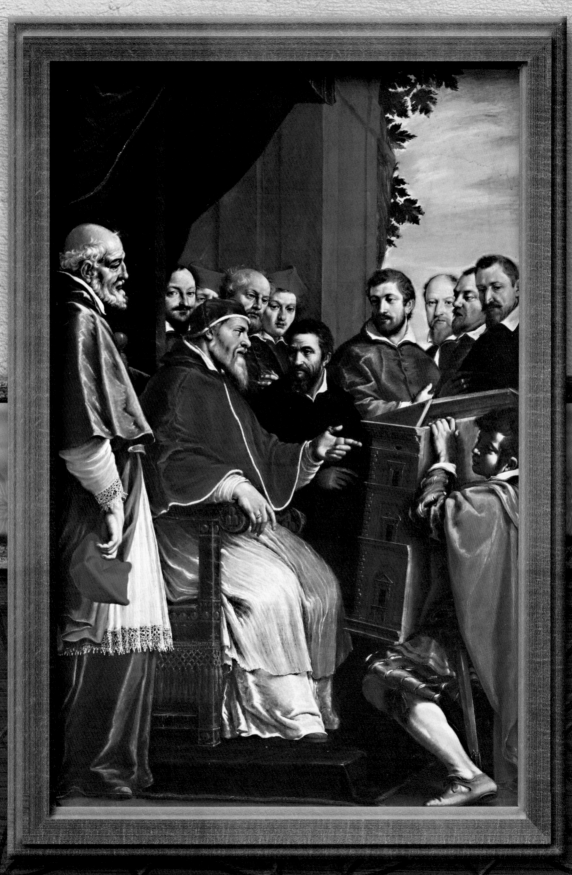

David

Above: Michelangelo made a number of pen and ink drawings of David, to try out different poses and to sketch out how he would carve the hero's face and muscles.

Previous page: In a painting by Fabrizio Boschi, Michelangelo (in the center, wearing black) presents a model of a building he has designed to Pope Julius II, his patron (seated).

His newfound fame meant that Michelangelo was soon in demand at home in Florence. Savonarola had become unpopular and been executed, so it now seemed safe to return. The cathedral authorities were talking about a giant statue of the great biblical hero David, who saved his people by killing the giant Goliath.

In the Fabrica del Duomo (Office of Cathedral Works), there was a block of marble. For years, people had talked of using it for the statue of David. Two sculptors, Duccio and Rossellino, had tried but their attempts had only succeeded in making the stone almost unusable.

Piero Soderini, who was now ruler of Florence, wanted to give the block to Leonardo da Vinci or another sculptor, Contucci. However, in 1501, the job of carving David finally went to Michelangelo because he had more experience working on large sculptures. Michelangelo and Leonardo were both great artists and people liked to draw comparisons between them. They did not argue over David, but there was sometimes rivalry.

August 16, 1501
Michelangelo is given a contract to produce a giant figure of David for Florence's cathedral.

January 1503
A meeting of citizens debates the positioning of the "David," which is still not finished.

A broken arm

In 1527, there were riots in Florence during the Italian Wars. A number of enemies of the Medici occupied the Palazzo della Signoria and threw things out of the windows at their enemies below. A bench that they hurled hit the statue of David and broke his raised arm. The writer and artist Vasari rescued the pieces so that the statue could later be mended.

In 1503, there was tension between them when they were commissioned to paint murals in the same room in the city hall. Neither artist finished the project.

"David" was a tough and lengthy job. Michelangelo had to choose a pose that fit in with the way the marble had already been worked. He could not show David in the traditional pose, with Goliath's head at his feet. Instead he decided to depict the hero as if he were eyeing the giant before the fight. The result was a triumph, and people were enthusiastic when the statue was finally unveiled in Florence in 1504.

However, Soderini told Michelangelo that the hero's nose was too broad. The sculptor was unwilling to be told what to do by a patron, so he took some marble dust in his hand, climbed up the scaffolding, and pretended to chisel at the nose. As Michelangelo let the dust fall to the ground, Soderini said that the nose was now much better.

Left: Michelangelo gave his "David" the strong, handsome features of a hero, but with a troubled expression, as if he truly is about to take on his enemy, Goliath.

1503
Michelangelo and Leonardo da Vinci are at work on paintings for Florence's city hall.

April 24, 1503
The wool merchants' guild commissions Michelangelo to carve statues of the 12 Apostles. Only St. Matthew was begun.

The Popes

The Renaissance popes were among the most powerful men in Europe. As the head of the church, the pope was first of all a religious leader, whom Christians believed had total authority in religious matters. He also had huge political power, controlling enormous lands in Italy, intervening in the affairs of European countries, commanding a large army, and sometimes claiming the right to appoint kings. The pope had access to the church's wealth, and this was often used to employ artists such as Michelangelo to produce works of religious art or to design churches and cathedrals. The popes were among Michelangelo's most important patrons, inviting him to work on exciting commissions but also frustrating him with their demands or their unwillingness to pay for his work.

Left: This document is an indulgence, which promised people who had given money to the church that they would spend less time in purgatory, the place where Catholics believe souls go before entering heaven.

Right: Many people thought that acquiring indulgences with money was wrong. Objections to the custom were one of the things that set off the Reformation, the movement that led to the founding of the Protestant churches. The Council of Trent (shown here) was a meeting of senior Catholic churchmen held many times from 1545 to 1563 to discuss how to react to the Protestants.

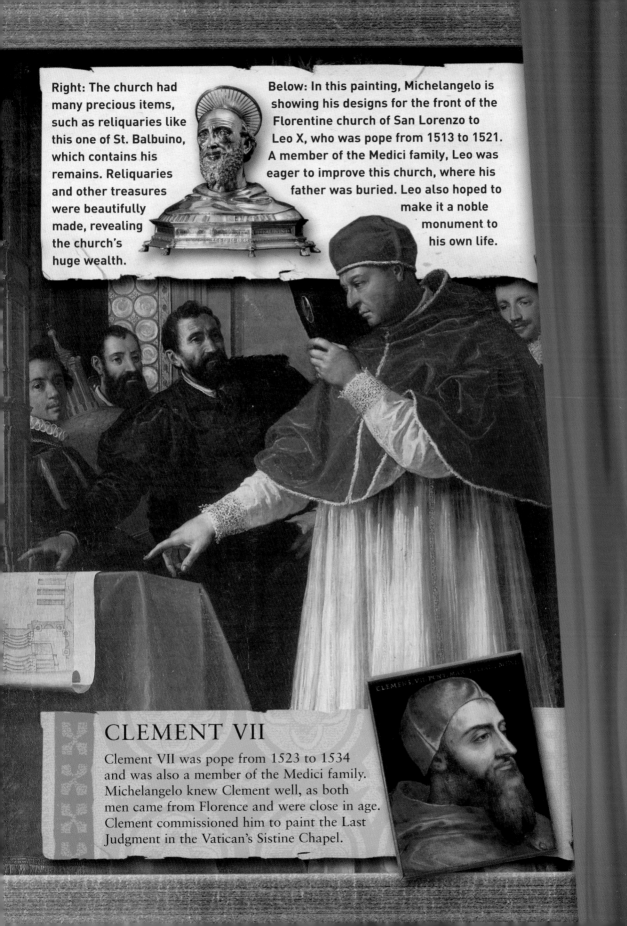

Right: The church had many precious items, such as reliquaries like this one of St. Balbuino, which contains his remains. Reliquaries and other treasures were beautifully made, revealing the church's huge wealth.

Below: In this painting, Michelangelo is showing his designs for the front of the Florentine church of San Lorenzo to Leo X, who was pope from 1513 to 1521. A member of the Medici family, Leo was eager to improve this church, where his father was buried. Leo also hoped to make it a noble monument to his own life.

CLEMENT VII

Clement VII was pope from 1523 to 1534 and was also a member of the Medici family. Michelangelo knew Clement well, as both men came from Florence and were close in age. Clement commissioned him to paint the Last Judgment in the Vatican's Sistine Chapel.

The Warrior Pope

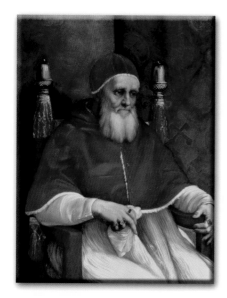

Above: Julius II was nearly 70 years old by the time Raphael painted his portrait, but his focused expression and his tense left hand still reveal the pope's powerful personality.

In 1503 a new pope was elected in Rome, Julius II. Julius's plans included some of the most ambitious works of art ever created, and he wanted Michelangelo, Italy's greatest sculptor, to be involved.

The previous pope, Alexander VI, had given away many of the papal lands to his Borgia relatives. Julius wanted to get these estates back, so that the papacy had a worldly power to match its spiritual importance. He also wanted to expel the French from Italy. Julius was even prepared to put on armor and go into battle to achieve his aims, an attitude that quickly won him the nickname "the warrior pope."

Julius had huge artistic ambitions. He knocked down the unstable fifth-century basilica of St. Peter's in the Vatican and began rebuilding the church on a much grander scale. At its center would be his own tomb—and this was to be designed and carved by Michelangelo. This was a vast project, intended to show the greatness of Julius as both a pope and a patron of the arts. It was to be three stories high and covered in life-size sculptures. Ordering and quarrying the marble alone took Michelangelo eight months.

November 1, 1503
Giuliano della Rovere is elected pope as Julius II. He aims to regain power over the lost papal lands.

March 1505
Michelangelo travels to Rome to begin work on the tomb of Julius II.

The project proved to be a disaster. Michelangelo was to work on it off and on for some 40 years. The work stopped and started for many reasons: when Michelangelo had a furious argument with the pope over money, when there were disagreements about the siting of the tomb, and when Michelangelo moved on to other projects.

In the end, the tomb was never finished the way Julius II intended. When the pope died in 1513, the design was scaled down by his successor, Leo X, and other carvers were employed to finish the job. The tomb was never even placed in St. Peter's, but in the much less grand church of San Pietro in Vincoli, also in Rome.

Above: The finished tomb of Julius II was smaller than planned, but still vast. Only three of the statues are by Michelangelo— the large, bearded Moses (bottom middle), and the figures of the biblical characters Rachel and Leah on either side.

"You've tried and tested the pope as not even the king of France would dare... we don't want to wage war with him over you and put our state at risk."

Piero Soderini, ruler of Florence, persuading Michelangelo to go back to work for Pope Julius II, 1506

April–November 1505
Michelangelo stays in Carrara, choosing marble and seeing that it is properly quarried and transported.

April–November 1506
Michelangelo is in dispute with Julius about the money needed for work and materials for his tomb.

Sistine Chapel

One of the most important parts of the Vatican is the Sistine Chapel, named after Pope Sixtus IV. Originally, the ceiling of the chapel was decorated with a pattern of gold stars. In 1508, Julius II decided that he would have it repainted with scenes from the Bible. Despite Michelangelo's lack of painting experience, Julius chose him to paint the ceiling.

It was a huge honor to be given such a high-profile commission. The pope had great painters such as Raphael to choose from, but he wanted Michelangelo. The sculptor had not worked on a fresco since he was an apprentice. But when a man as important as Julius II insisted, it was hard to refuse. Michelangelo worked on the ceiling from 1508 to 1512. It took a long time for several reasons. Most importantly, it was a huge project with lots of figures. Another problem was money. At one point, Michelangelo stopped work to beg the pope for funds to complete the task. It was difficult work. The figures were designed to be seen from the chapel floor, but Michelangelo had to paint high up on scaffolding. This made it difficult for the artist to see how work was progressing.

Right: Michelangelo showed Adam just at the moment when he is brought to life by God.

1508
Michelangelo begins work on the Sistine Chapel ceiling.

September 1, 1512
The Medici family returns to Florence after Soderini falls from power.

It also made it harder to tell whether the figures had the proper proportions.

According to the biographer Condivi, Michelangelo worked on his own, applying the plaster, mixing the colors, and doing all the painting. But this is unlikely as frescoes were very time-consuming and required the work of a whole team of people. In fact, the artist recorded payments to various other men, probably including a plasterer.

Mold attack

In the winter of 1508, ugly marks appeared all over the Sistine Chapel painting. The architect Giuliano da Sangallo had seen a similar problem before and came to advise Michelangelo. A mold was growing on the plaster and Sangallo showed the artist how to remove it.

The results were breathtaking—a range of biblical scenes, including God's creation of man and woman. The artist's use of perspective and his dramatic painting of the figures were admired by everyone who saw it.

October 1, 1512
The scaffolding in the Sistine Chapel is taken down to reveal the newly decorated ceiling.

March 9, 1513
Leo X (a member of the Medici family) is elected pope after the death of Julius II.

A New Challenge

After finishing the Sistine Chapel ceiling, Michelangelo went back to work on Julius's tomb. In spite of his fame, he was facing problems with his work. His family still asked him for money. Then he was offered two projects that took him in a new direction—he became an architect.

Below: For the Medici library, Michelangelo designed white walls with details highlighted with dark stone. This style of decoration was soon copied by many other builders.

After Julius's death in 1513, Michelangelo had many arguments over the money for the still unfinished tomb. He also started a number of projects that fell through. In addition, he had an argument with his father, who mistakenly thought that Michelangelo had had him thrown out of his house in Florence.

1516
A new contract is drawn up for Michelangelo for a revised design of the tomb of Julius II.

1517–18
Michelangelo makes several trips to Carrara to get marble for the tomb of Julius II.

Book collectors

Printing with movable type was invented in the 1440s. Before this date, books had to be copied by hand, so they were rare and expensive. By Michelangelo's time, there were printing presses all over Europe, and rich and educated people liked to fill their own libraries with beautiful books.

Meanwhile, in Florence the Medici family had returned to power once more. Cardinal Giulio de' Medici was building a new chapel and library onto the church of San Lorenzo and asked Michelangelo to design them. The chapel was to house four tombs for the Medici family, while the library was to contain the family's collection of books and manuscripts. Michelangelo seized the opportunity to get away from the problems with Julius's tomb. He returned to Florence and threw himself into the design of these two buildings.

Michelangelo began work on the Medici chapel in 1519 and, over the next few years, agreed on the plans for the library with Giulio, who became Pope Clement VII in 1523. Both buildings took years to complete and are stunning designs. In the chapel, the artist used his decorative scheme as a framework for the statues and tombs. In the library, he invented entirely new forms of decoration, such as designs for columns that later architects copied.

Michelangelo was now at the height of his creative powers, but crisis was about to strike his home city once more.

Fire safety

Clement VII took a detailed interest in the library designs. He even asked Michelangelo to give the room below a stone-vaulted ceiling. His reason was that, if a fire started accidentally downstairs, the flames would not be able to spread and burn the books in the library above.

November 19, 1523
Giulio de' Medici is elected pope as Clement VII.

1524
Michelangelo is commissioned to build the new Laurentian Library at San Lorenzo, Florence.

War!

Above: Michelangelo sketched out new designs for Florence's fortifications in drawings. The walls had star-shaped platforms from which guns could be aimed in many different directions.

In 1527, the Italian cities were in trouble as armies from France and the Holy Roman Empire (Germany and Spain) invaded. Rome was looted and burned. The people of Florence threw out the Medici again. Pope Clement VII, who was a Medici himself, backed the Holy Roman Emperor when he besieged Florence.

Michelangelo was a loyal Florentine citizen who loved his home city, but he also worked for the Medici and the pope. He found himself in a difficult position. Should he back his fellow citizens or side with the pope and the Medici? He soon decided on loyalty to his home city and started to design new fortifications to help protect Florence.

To begin with, Michelangelo worked without pay or contract. He knew that the important thing was to act quickly, because the city's defenses were in urgent need of upgrading. So he worked hard, but his position was difficult because Malatesta Baglione, the commander of the Florentine army, thought that Michelangelo was a Medici spy. By September 1529, Michelangelo had had enough of the accusations. Sick of the lies of Baglione and his friends, he left Florence, making for northern Italy.

1527
The holy city of Rome is invaded and looted. The Medici are again expelled from Florence.

July 2, 1528
Michelangelo's favorite brother, Buonarroto, dies of the plague.

The Florentines begged Michelangelo to come back. He returned in November, working for another eight months to try to keep the enemy out of the city. Eventually, the city fell after a long struggle. The enemy rushed into Florence, killing and arresting citizens as they went. Michelangelo feared for his life.

The artist went into hiding and concealed himself in a tiny crypt under the altar in the Medici Chapel in San Lorenzo. No one knew about the hiding place except for one friend, who fed Michelangelo until the pope announced that the artist should be allowed to go free. His hiding place was so cramped and secret that its location was only discovered by accident in 1975.

Friends and assistants

Most Renaissance artists had young assistants, known as *garzoni*. Although he did not have a large workshop with many *garzoni*, Michelangelo had a number of assistants over the years. Some of them, like Pietro Urbano, who joined him in 1515, became good friends and stayed with him for years.

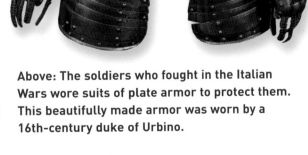

Above: The soldiers who fought in the Italian Wars wore suits of plate armor to protect them. This beautifully made armor was worn by a 16th-century duke of Urbino.

1529	October 1529–August 1530
Michelangelo is appointed governor of fortifications for the city of Florence.	Florence is under siege by the troops of Holy Roman Emperor Charles V, who rules Germany and Spain.

THE LATER
YEARS

4

Michelangelo the Poet

Previous page: The figure of the old man Nicodemus in the "Pietà" in Florence cathedral is a self-portrait. Michelangelo did not finish this sculpture because of a flaw in the marble.

Michelangelo wrote poetry throughout his life, but most of his surviving poems date from the 1530s onward. This was also the period when he left his hometown, never to return: In 1534 he moved to Rome to continue his work for the popes.

Some of Michelangelo's poems were vivid accounts of things that happened in his life and work. One of the most famous describes how uncomfortable he was when painting the Sistine Chapel ceiling, bent almost double, with paint splashing on his face. He said that it was no wonder he sometimes got his perspective wrong when he was on all fours and could not see what he was doing.

In the 1530s, Michelangelo met a highly cultured nobleman, Tommaso de' Cavalieri, and a woman who was a campaigner for religious reform, Vittoria Colonna. Tommaso so impressed Michelangelo that the artist gave his friend some of his finest drawings.

Left: This portrait of Michelangelo by Marcello Venusti shows the artist in his 50s, at the time when he wrote many of his greatest poems.

1532
Alessandro de' Medici becomes ruler of Florence, following the end of the siege of the city.

October 13, 1534
Paul III (family name Alessandro Farnese) is elected pope after the death of Clement VII.

"New" poetry

Michelangelo's poetry is still read today, partly because it seems very modern. It can be hard to understand, but it is also very powerful. Michelangelo had a passionate interest in language. He liked to use puns (playing on different meanings of the same word), and he often broke the rules of grammar intentionally.

Michelangelo was never interested in getting married or having children. Vittoria became a close friend purely because she inspired him with her spiritual quality and religious beliefs.

As he got older, Michelangelo wrote more religious poems, many of which were inspired by Vittoria's ideas. He wrote that the love of God was even more important to him than the art he had created throughout his life. The poems were not published in Michelangelo's lifetime. They were intended to be passed around among his friends—many were even jotted down on the same sheets of paper as his drawings. In 1623, the artist's great-nephew, Michelangelo Buonarroti il Giovane, published a collection of them. Ever since, Michelangelo has been valued as one of the best Italian poets.

> *"With pen and colors you have shown how art*
> *Can equal nature. Also in a sense*
> *You have from nature snatched her eminence,*
> *Making the painted beauty touch the heart."*

Michelangelo writing about how art can be as powerful as nature, in "To Giorgio Vasari," his friend and the author of *Lives of the Artists*

1535
Michelangelo is commissioned by the pope to paint the Last Judgment on the wall of the Sistine Chapel.

1536
Michelangelo first meets his friend Vittoria Colonna.

Michelangelo's Beliefs

During the Renaissance, artists argued endlessly about whether painting or sculpture was the greater art form. Michelangelo believed that it was the ideas behind the work that were important together with the skill with which they were expressed, not the art form the artist chose. This was a new idea at the time and it showed that an artist's own thoughts were important and that an artist could express his own beliefs and ideas, not just those of his patron. As Michelangelo grew older, however, his thoughts turned more and more toward traditional Christian beliefs. He saw his work as a way of expressing his deep Christian faith.

Right: Baldassare Castiglione (1478–1529) wrote a book called *The Courtier*, in which he taught people how the perfect, educated Renaissance gentleman should behave. He was a huge influence on Renaissance Italy.

A SPIRITUAL LADY

One of Michelangelo's closest friends was named Vittoria Colonna. She had been the wife of a successful military leader, the Marquis of Pescara. When he died, she decided to devote her time to religion. She wrote religious poetry and was one of a group of thinkers who tried to encourage understanding between Protestants and Catholics. Michelangelo admired her, wrote poems to her, and gave her many of his drawings. When she died in 1547, he was said to have been grief-stricken.

Right: Michelangelo painted this image of Mary, Joseph, and Jesus in the early 1500s. The painting may have been produced for the marriage of two nobles, Agnolo Doni and Maddalena Strozzi, in 1504. No one knows for sure the meaning of the naked figures in the background, but they may represent the time before Jesus' birth and Christianity became a world religion. If this is the case, the painting expresses the artist's belief in the importance of the Christian age in which he lived.

Left: The philosopher Marsilio Ficino was popular at the Medici court in Florence. He introduced Italians to the thinking of the ancient Greek philosopher Plato, especially the idea that outer beauty and inner holiness might go together. This appealed to Michelangelo especially, who often painted his religious figures with extreme beauty.

Troubled Times

People were shocked by the burning of Rome during the Italian Wars. Many thought it was God's punishment on the pope for his luxurious lifestyle. So to show his seriousness, in the early 1530s Pope Clement VII asked Michelangelo to paint a somber picture in the Sistine Chapel.

Left: The "Last Judgment" impressed viewers by its sheer size, but the nakedness of the swirling bodies in the painting shocked many people. Clothing was added to the figures in the late 16th century.

The subject Clement chose was the Last Judgment, when many Christians believe that Jesus will judge the souls of the living and the dead. Michelangelo painted this behind the altar, where it would be the focus for anyone visiting the chapel.

Precious colors

Renaissance artists made their colors by mixing minerals with oil or water. Some of the minerals, such as lapis lazuli, which was used to make blue, were rare. Blue was therefore used sparingly and was often reserved for the clothing of important people.

1537
Pope Paul III releases Michelangelo from working on Julius II's tomb so he can concentrate on the "Last Judgment."

1537
Alessandro de' Medici is assassinated by political opponents, and Cosimo de' Medici becomes ruler of Florence.

The Reformation

In the early 16th century, the Roman Catholic Church was under attack from many people who thought it had moved away from the core beliefs of Christianity. This movement was called the Reformation, and especially in northern Europe, it led to the formation of new, Protestant, churches. Protestants believed that the authority of the Bible was more important than that of the pope. Catholics felt threatened by this questioning of the pope's authority.

The painting took around six years to finish, including a year at the beginning while the wall was being prepared. Michelangelo worked with only one assistant, Antonio, who ground his colors and helped to apply the plaster to each section of wall before he began to paint it. By 1534, there was a new pope, Paul III, who was just as eager to see the work completed as Clement had been. Paul visited the chapel with one of his officials in February 1537. The official, Biagio de Cesena, protested that there were too many naked figures in the painting. Michelangelo got revenge for this interference by painting Biagio as one of the figures at the mouth of hell.

Michelangelo finally completed the enormous painting in 1541. Again, some people, including friends of Biagio, complained about the naked figures. However, many visitors were overwhelmed by the huge picture and its cascades of swirling figures, many of them in positions that seemed almost impossible to draw. Vasari, author of *Lives of the Artists*, was full of praise, believing that the painting could move anyone, whether or not they knew anything about art: "he shakes the hearts of all who are not knowledgeable as well as those who are knowledgeable in such matters." As time went by, more and more onlookers saw the fresco as a triumph.

March 1538
Michelangelo is commissioned by Pope Paul III to remodel the buildings on Rome's Capitoline Hill.

October 31, 1541
The "Last Judgment" is formally unveiled in the Sistine Chapel.

Master Architect

After completing the "Last Judgment," Michelangelo was busy with other work for the pope, including paintings for the Vatican's Pauline Chapel and finally finishing Julius II's tomb. Then came his biggest challenge of all. The pope made Michelangelo chief architect of the continuing rebuilding of St. Peter's. It was the most important church in the Western world.

Above: This painting by Passignano shows Michelangelo (in black) presenting his model of St. Peter's to the pope (in white) to show his patron how the finished building would look.

Michelangelo was more than 70 when he was made chief architect of St. Peter's in 1546. He was taking on Europe's biggest building project, which had already been led by some of the best artists of the time. The project's most recent chief had been Antonio da Sangallo, who had just died.

Michelangelo disliked Sangallo's design and demolished a lot of the work that had already been built. He came up with a new plan, a new front entrance, and a new design for the dome.

1546
Michelangelo is made chief architect of St. Peter's and commissioned to complete the Farnese Palace in Rome.

1550
Lives of the Artists by Giorgio Vasari is published. The section on Michelangelo is the only one on a living artist.

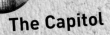

The Capitol

The Capitoline Hill is one of the seven hills on which Rome is built. It had been the religious heart of ancient Rome, the city's center of government in the Middle Ages, and was one of the most important parts of the city.

Once more, Michelangelo had to put up with delays and criticisms. Some complained about the waste of money caused by the changes in plan; others objected that the new building was too dark; still others disliked the decoration. Even with the pope's support, St. Peter's took decades to finish. Later architects changed many details of the design, so the building seen today, finally completed in the 17th century, is different from Michelangelo's plans.

Meanwhile, Michelangelo took on two other building projects. He won a competition to complete another building that had been left unfinished by Sangallo's death: the Farnese Palace, home of Pope Paul III's family. He modified Sangallo's design and added little touches, such as a row of amusing masks carved in stone. He also worked on building designs for Rome's Capitoline Hill, where he created an elegant square as a fitting centerpiece to the city.

Right: The dome of St. Peter's was completed by Giacomo della Porta. Della Porta altered the design of Michelangelo's original, but it still has its grandeur.

1552
The stairway leading up to Michelangelo's elegant square on the Capitoline Hill in Rome is completed.

1553
Ascanio Condivi's *Life of Michelangelo Buonarroti* is published.

Last Years

Michelangelo was by now respected as one of Europe's greatest artists. However, his success had not come easily. He had fought to work in the way he wanted and even to get paid. More than once he had become involved in political and military events when he would rather have been drawing or carving.

In his old age, these struggles continued. He carried on as chief architect at St. Peter's, in spite of the fact that several changes of popes meant that his contract was often rewritten. There were also several occasions when he did not get paid. He drew designs for many other buildings as well, including the church of the Florentines in Rome.

Meanwhile, he worked on carvings of one of his favorite themes, the subject that had made him famous, the pietà. One of his late "Pietàs" includes a figure of Nicodemus, one of the men who took Christ's body down from the cross.

Left: Michelangelo's last work, the "Rondanini Pietà," was left unfinished at his death. The partly carved figures seem to be emerging from the marble.

1555
Michelangelo is grief-stricken at the death of his servant and assistant Francesco d'Amadore Urbino.

1559
Michelangelo draws up plans for the church of the Florentine community in Rome.

Left: This painting by Agostino Ciampelli shows Michelangelo's funeral, which was held in the church of San Lorenzo in Florence. Many Florentines attended, and the writer Benedetto Varchi made a speech in tribute to the "divine Michelangelo."

Michelangelo's Nicodemus is a self-portrait (*see page 47*). He hoped that this sculpture would be used on his tomb, but while he was working on it he found a flaw in the marble, lost his temper, and abandoned the work.

The Florentines tried to encourage Michelangelo to come back to his home city. He resisted, however, and stayed in Rome to continue his architectural work, even though his old enemy Biagio was still trying to get him dismissed.

On February 12, 1564, while working on one of his "Pietàs," the artist began to feel feverish. He was soon in bed and, in spite of the efforts of his doctors, died on February 18. His friend Tommaso de' Cavalieri and his servant Antonio, who had helped him with the "Last Judgment," were among those by his bedside. He had asked that his body be taken back to Florence—the great artist would go home at last.

Medicines

In Michelangelo's time, doctors used medicines made of herbs and other natural ingredients. The artist's doctor, Antonio del Francese, gave him medicines made of honey, vinegar, and seawater, together with almonds. None of these were any use in curing the fever.

1561

Michelangelo's model for the dome of St. Peter's is completed.

February 18, 1564

Michelangelo dies in his house in the Piazza Marcel de' Corvi in Rome.

Michelangelo's Legacy

Above: Drawings like this "ideal head" show Michelangelo's mastery at drawing human features. He was single-minded in his search for artistic perfection.

Michelangelo's place in history as one of the greatest artists of all time was already certain during his own lifetime. No one else, except for his contemporary Leonardo da Vinci, had excelled in so many different art forms. For generations of artists since his death, he has come to stand for the perfect artistic genius.

Michelangelo's greatest legacy is his surviving works that we can see today—the sculptures, paintings, and buildings. These works have been an inspiration to other artists, many of whom have measured the quality of their own works by comparing them with Michelangelo's. Few people before or since have made such lifelike drawings of the human form, produced sculptures with such perfect surfaces, or made so many large paintings with such complete mastery of perspective and composition.

The beauty of his work can still be a surprise. When experts finished cleaning the Sistine Chapel ceiling in 1994, its colors looked much brighter than before. Suddenly, people saw how the paintings must have appeared when they were new. People understood the amazement of those who first saw the artist's work in the 16th century.

July 14, 1564
An elaborate funeral is held for Michelangelo in Florence.

1590
The dome of St. Peter's is finally completed, but Michelangelo's design has been altered.

As a result of Michelangelo's work, the role of the artist changed forever. Before Michelangelo, the artist was the servant of his employer who was there to produce exactly what the patron wanted and rarely dared argue about it. Michelangelo stood up to his patrons and refused to make every change that they requested. He realized that an artist can have a unique vision—something that he or she has to express—and no patron, even a pope or a king, should stand in his or her way.

Michelangelo's struggles were worth it in the end: They allowed him to share his vision and helped later artists gain the freedom to follow in his footsteps and do the same. Every Western artist, from the 16th century to today, is in his debt.

Right: When tourists flock to Florence to see the Renaissance art, the statue "David" is the image they instantly recognize. It is the statue among the thousands of marble figures that they most want to see.

1623
Michelangelo's great-nephew, Michelangelo Buonarroti il Giovane, publishes 137 of the artist's poems.

1980–94
The Sistine Chapel ceiling is cleaned, revealing its bright colors for the first time in more than 400 years.

Glossary

anatomy the study of the shape and structure of a plant or animal, especially of the human body.

apprentice a person who enters into a legal agreement with someone to work for a set period of time. In return, the apprentice is taught an art or craft.

Bacchus the ancient Greek god of wine and pleasure.

cardinal one of the senior priests of the Roman Catholic Church. The cardinals make up the body of people who elect a new pope.

cartoon in Renaissance art, a detailed working drawing that is made for a painting; it is usually drawn at the same size as the finished work.

centaur in Greek and Roman mythology, a creature with the head and torso of a man and the body and legs of a horse.

classical referring to the civilizations of ancient Greece and Rome, and, in particular, their culture, art, and architecture.

commission to employ an artist, builder, or craftsman to create something. In Michelangelo's day, commissions were handed out by wealthy people who were called patrons.

contract a formal agreement made between two people. It is usually written down, signed by both people, and is enforceable by law.

courtier a person who is a member of the social circle of a prince or ruler; courtiers include the noblemen and women who attend the ruler, but who are not the ruler's paid servants.

crucifix an image of Christ on the cross.

crypt the underground or basement story of a building, especially a basement in a church that is used for burials.

Cupid the ancient Roman god of love, sometimes shown as a winged boy carrying a bow and arrow.

dowry the money or property that a woman or her family traditionally gives to her husband at their wedding.

faun in Roman mythology, a god of the countryside. A faun is often shown in artworks with a man's body but with some goatlike features such as tail, ears, and hooves.

Florentine a person who lives in the Italian city of Florence.

fresco an image that has been painted onto a wall when the plaster is still damp.

garzoni the apprentices and assistants in the workshop of a Renaissance artist.

gonfalonier the title given to some rulers of the city of Florence.

guild a group of people, usually belonging to the same trade or profession, who band together to protect their common interests.

ideal head a painting, drawing, or sculpture of a human head with perfect proportions. It is meant to demonstrate the correct way of drawing the human features.

Last Judgment in Christian belief, the final judgment by God of human souls, that happens at the end of the world.

manuscript book, document, or other text that has been written out by hand.

Mass the central rite of the Roman Catholic Church, in which bread wafers and wine, believed to take the form of the body and blood of Christ, are taken by the priest and members of the congregation. It is known in other Christian churches as the Eucharist or the Lord's Supper.

Medieval something that relates to the Middle Ages.

Middle Ages a period in history from about the 5th century to the 14th century.

movable type small, reusable metal letters that were used in the early printing presses; the key technology that led to the production and distribution of printed books in the 15th century.

mural painting made directly onto the surface of a wall.

panel painting painting made on a solid material, such as a piece of wood.

patron a person who employs an artist.

perspective a method of showing three-dimensional distance in a two-dimensional painting or drawing, using techniques such as making more distant objects look smaller than those closer to the artist.

podestà an official in a Renaissance Italian town or village who combined the roles of judge and mayor.

prior the assistant head in a Roman Catholic monastery or abbey who ranks just below the abbot.

relic in the Roman Catholic Church, a part of a saint's body or something that was used by or linked with a saint. A relic is considered very holy and is usually kept in a special ornate container called a reliquary.

relief a carved panel in which the figures or other main subjects stand only slightly raised from the background.

Renaissance a movement in art, literature, and science in which a rediscovery of the classical cultures of the ancient world led to a rebirth of culture. It involved developments such as greater realism in painting. It started in 14th-century Italy and gradually spread throughout Europe.

shrine a church, chapel, or similar sacred space dedicated to a specific saint and often containing the tomb or relics of that saint.

St. Peter's the church in the Vatican in Rome that is the headquarters of the Roman Catholic Church.

Vatican the pope's residence and home of the central governing body of the Roman Catholic Church. Today, the Vatican is in Vatican City, a tiny independent state ruled by the pope and located within Rome, Italy.

vault an arched structure, usually made of stone or brick, forming the ceiling of a church or other building.

Bibliography

The Architecture of Michelangelo, Ackerman, James, published by Penguin, 1970

Michelangelo: A Biography, Bull, George, published by Viking, 1995

Michelangelo: Life, Letters, and Poetry, Bull, George, published by Oxford University Press, 1997

Michelangelo, Hibberd, Howard, published by Allen Lane, 1975

Michelangelo and the Pope's Ceiling, King, Ross, published by Walker & Co., 2003

Michelangelo: His Life, Work, and Times, Murray, Linda, published by Thames & Hudson, 1984

The Little Book of Michelangelo, Sueur, Hélène, et al, published by Flammarion, 2003

Lives of the Artists, Vasari, Giorgio, published by Penguin, 1965

Sources of quotes:

p.15 *Michelangelo: Life, Letters, and Poetry,* George Bull, 1997

p.29 *Michelangelo: Life, Letters, and Poetry,* George Bull, 1997

p.39 *Michelangelo: A Biography,* George Bull, 1995

p.49 *The Sonnets of Michelangelo,* translated by Elizabeth Jennings, Carcanet Press, Manchester, 1998

Some web sites that will help you explore Michelangelo's world:

www.artcyclopedia.com/artists/michelangelo_ buonarroti.html
Michelangelo Buonarroti Online: A guide to museums where Michelangelo's works may be seen.

www.michelangelo.com/buonarroti.html
Michelangelo Buonarroti: Comprehensive coverage of the artist and his life.

Index